The Goal Digger

How to Rock your Network Marketing

Biz on Social Media

"Making the rest of my life, the best of my life."

Kimberly Olson, PhD

The Goal Digger

How to Rock your Network Marketing

Biz on Social Media

CONTENTS

FORWARD

"Success in this industry is not in finding the right person, but in becoming the right person."
–Dr. Forrest Shaklee, Founder of Shaklee

It wouldn't have been possible for me to grow my network marketing business without knowing the power of having an abundant mindset. When I first started in this business, I have to admit I was fearful, and had some doubts. I wondered how I could make the adjustment to this type of work and what I would tell my family and friends. The fear of failure kept me paralyzed at times and I found it was difficult for me to get into activity.

It wasn't until one day when I went for a walk on a beautiful sunny day that it just hit me. I realized that If I continued to replay the story of fear, self-doubt, and possible failure in my mind it would basically be impossible for me to move forward and do the necessary action steps needed to create any success.

I made the decision that day to start working more on my mindset. I did this by thinking of three things I was already grateful for, saying affirmations and visualizing daily. Through this process I was able to gain more confidence which allowed me to do the daily action steps needed to reach my goals.

I was then able to reach the top of my company in under one year and become a top income earner. Mindset was and still is definitely my foundation. It has supported me in my journey in creating the lifestyle and freedom-based business I have always dreamed of.

One of the most valuable lessons I have learned in this business is that you don't have to reinvent the wheel, you just have to follow the proven system, and Kimberly's training does just that. I have shared several of Kimberly's trainings with my team and it has definitely made an impact in their success.

I love how her way of teaching is broken down into powerful yet easy to follow steps that work! She utilizes both the mindset aspect along with the daily action steps needed to create a very successful network marketing business.

This book can definitely impact your life in a positive way that will allow you to have a successful network marketing business and teach others to do the same.

Bright Blessings & Massive Success,
Kristi Dear
International Success & Mindset Coach
KristiDear.com

GOAL DIGGER DEDICATION

It's one thing to follow me on social media but a whole other ball game to be married to me so that is why this book is dedicated to my amazing husband, Scott. He has and always will be my biggest supporter and the one who encourages me to go after my dreams, no matter how crazy they are. There are a lot of risks I've asked him to take and he has trusted me every step of the way. I love you, Sweetie!

I would like to thank my father-in-law, Greg, for his constant encouragement. To my assistants, Anna Barefield and Leslie Ridl, I'm not sure where I'd be if it weren't for your organization and commitment. Victoria Alexander, thank you for not giving up on me and getting me to finally take a look at your network marketing opportunity – you changed my life. And of course, I wouldn't be here without my Rockstar team members, specifically my leaders Kristi Dully, Janya Joy and Leann Johnson – I love you guys!

And I'd like to give a special shout out to all my bootcampers, especially my original crew: Tonya Ransbottom-Luna, Charlotte LoSasso, Lindsay Sewell, Tammie Land, Chiara Reese, Pam Satterwhite Kessel, Ginnie Busbey, Dina Robinson, Cassie Meister, Laura J. LaRosa, Linda Eskridge, Missy Herguth, Jeanine Risk, Heidi Gardner, Patti Edwards, Dawn Kosma, Avoree Gore, Stacy L. Newman, Brytanny Price, Gayle Jones, Jennifer Skomski, Kim Stevens, Janelle Baker, Brigid Peddy, Missy Kennedy, Jamie Babbini, Jessica Johnson, Claudia Garcia-Caffarella, Deanna Baldwin, Amanda Watson, Paula Dempsey, Amber Worner, Sandra Burlison, Hayley Sirimalalak, Maria Kilroy, Melynda Fitt, Shevaun Strickland, Angela Battle, Erin Grimes, Katharine M. Pierce, Suzette Nava, Stacy Jankowski, Candi Pardue, Beth Dorsett, Suzanne E. Taylor, Suzanne Burgess, Jeanie Hutchins, Amie Clark, Chariti Kupiec, Jessica Parrott, Tina Thomas, Tiffany Wilkins-Alexander, Veronica Sheeler, Amanda Woodland, Jaya Es, Megan Guertin,

Amanda Jean DiPietro and Lyla Widick. Thank you for trusting me as your leader!

INTRODUCTION

"The greatest benefit isn't getting what you want. The greatest benefit is what you'll need to become in order to get what you want. The journey is everything." ~ Eric Worre

I'm guessing if you're reading this, you most likely discovered me online by watching one of my Facebook or Instagram Lives, participating in my workshops or by signing up for my small group coaching bootcamps. No matter how we've become connected, I'm so thankful and grateful you've decided to let me into your life as your coach and hopefully as your friend. I've always had a passion for teaching and leading others and I'm excited to embark on this journey together!

I'd like to start by sharing my story with you because although I've found success through several businesses, it wasn't always that way for me. So, no matter where you're at, whether you're just starting out or feel that you're limping along not making any progress, I completely understand. I went many, many years without making a dime so just hang in there and know that anything is possible if you stick with it and keep your eye on your dreams.

In 2011, I launched my first blog *FitKim.com* with the hopes of building a business through selling meal plans and making income from ads and affiliate marketing. I made some progress here and there but never enough financially to contribute in a meaningful way. I did learn a *ton* because I self-taught myself everything from building a website to being able to speak to an audience comfortably and share my passion and enthusiasm.

While working full time as the years went along, I invested thousands and thousands of dollars in coaching and by buying online programs. I seriously did every single thing they said but I never made my initial investment back and found myself with a pile of credit card bills and so much frustration I pretty much gave up. Oh,

I also had two precious baby girls 19 months apart so that also took up a lot of my focus😊.

A few weeks before Elise was born, my boss at the time flew out to Austin to spend the day in my sales territory. She ended the visit by letting me know the company wasn't doing well financially and had to let me go. I'm pretty sure that's the most afraid I've been in my entire life. You can't exactly go out and interview like a champ when you're almost nine months pregnant!

What followed was five long months of unemployment, stress, worry and more and more credit card bills piling up. I don't think I had one good night's sleep during that time and it wasn't just the newborn's fault. I was feeling so hopeless and as though I'd let my family down. I was a complete failure. I'd wasted so much of our money trying to get my little side gig going and now we were in a big financial mess. I've always struggled with anxiety and depression and I was at my all-time low. Wine o'clock couldn't come soon enough in my household.

Eventually I found a job but because of all the months of not working, we weren't making ends meet and we were definitely not getting ahead. You may not know this but childcare in Austin is one of the highest in the country. I'm so thankful every single day for God blessing us with our girls but I didn't have the foresight to know how expensive they would be! I really didn't know how to fix it and kept praying for God to show me a better way.

A good friend of mine, Victoria, reached out to me about a new network marketing company she'd recently joined and told me she was having a blast and making a ton of money. To be completely honest, I didn't believe a word she'd said. This was the *fourth* company she'd approached me about and had said the same thing about all of them. Well maybe not the money part but she did talk them all up so I was a bit jaded. I told her it wasn't the right time for me and we left it at that. But the girl is very persistent so it wasn't long before she'd reach back out again.

We ran into each other a few months later at a girls' night and she was even more excited than the last time I'd talked to her about her network marketing company. I was still hesitant but she asked me if I'd try the product and tell her what I thought. She's so smart – ha! So of course I tried it and loved it right away. I was for sure interested in ordering it but she kept asking me about selling it.

I'd tried other companies before and was not successful at them. But something inside of me said, "*What if? What if you don't try it? And what do you have to lose?*" I told her that if I didn't make my initial investment back by the time my credit card statement came, I was out. And so I began. Well sort of began. I tripped, and stumbled…a lot and looking back, I spammed a ton of my friends. It's so embarrassing to think about it but I know I had to go through the wrong way to do it to become so passionate about teaching the right way to do it.

The first few months were okay and I did see success based on the company's newbie standards. But after I'd exhausted my warm market, I felt pretty lost. I watched every single training I could find on Facebook or YouTube from leaders in my company but no one I could see was sharing step-by-step how to build your business online. I knew it could be done and it made so much sense to me that I just had to figure it out.

I hired some coaches and took as many online programs as I could afford and would implement what I was learning right away. Once I started getting the hang of attraction marketing and became consistent on social media, that's when my business completely exploded. My friends list went from 200 to 5,000 in just a few short months, my Instagram broke 10,000 followers and my Facebook Lives were ranging from 2,000 to 7,000+ views. And it started to become really fun!

Since then, I've continued to build my network marketing business so I can stay completely in the trenches of the industry as well as stay attuned to all the changes that are constantly happening on social media. I do private business coaching for network marketers as well as run online bootcamps and workshops. In addition, our family has become debt free and it makes me so dedicated and committed to helping my followers embrace the same type of financial freedom that I now have. I was finally able to quit the corporate world once and for all and now get the most peaceful sleep that you could imagine.

The bottom line is that entrepreneurs are very creative but this also makes them a bit disorganized and kind of all over the place. With that being said, having a system to follow that you can not only put in place for your own business, but to be able to turn around and teach to your team, that's where the magic and the power of duplication falls into place.

Thank you from the bottom of my heart for trusting me and allowing me to be your teacher – I promise you that I will do everything in my power to support you on your journey to success. I know you have what it takes to go after your dreams, crush your goals and create the life you've always wanted and I'm going to do whatever I can to help you get there! Stay committed, work through this book and then turn around and teach this to your team. You're going to be absolutely blown away at the transformation. Now let's do this!

CHAPTER 1

Stepping into Prosperity
and an Abundant Mindset

"Whatever the mind can conceive and believe, it can achieve." ~Napoleon Hill

I know you're excited right now but as time goes along, that excitement might waiver as life gets in the way and you may find yourself saying you don't have enough time to do the action steps at the end of each chapter. In my experience, this is the old version of yourself trying to pull you back into old habits and stop you from growing. This is what it means to be "stuck." However, I'm going to challenge you to find the time no matter what it takes because you need to do that to break through where you're at now and take it to the next level. No excuses, deal?

If you've been following me for any length of time, you know I'm big on setting goals and finding a strong "why." If we don't know what we're working towards, it makes it really hard to get up in the morning with a spring in our step or stay up late when we really just want to crawl into bed.

If you've ever struggled with procrastination or lack of motivation in your business, it's most likely because you either didn't clearly define your goals or your why wasn't strong enough to keep you going. When you see successful people around you in your company or on social media that are just driven and going for it, they have a super strong why and clear goals. You need that too so let's start there!

Your Why

In a couple of sentences, write down why you joined this business. Did you want more time freedom, extra income or just something to call your own? Whatever it is, it should make your heart feel good and put a smile on your face. Instead of just writing out the facts, put meaning behind it such as "*I want to be able to drop my girls off at school every day and pick them up so that I can see them as much as possible while they are still young and growing so fast. I don't want to miss anything! I want to bring in enough extra income each month so that I don't feel the burden of our debt on my shoulders and can sleep soundly at night. A romantic vacation away would be nice too!"*

Write your why:

_____

_____

_____

_____

_____

_____

_____

_____

_____

Creating Goals that Matter

I've been all about goal setting since I was a teenager, but it wasn't until I learned how to make sure that they were tied back to my why did I really come to love not only the process but the end results. Have you ever achieved something only to feel let down or empty inside afterwards? That's because it wasn't super important to you in a meaningful way.

When it comes to goal setting, we're going to follow something I learned from Tony Robbin's in his program, *The Time of Your Life*. It's pretty elaborate so I've simplified the process here to make sure that this is something you can do and also duplicate for your team. We're going to look at what you'd like to create personally and professionally in your life because both are equally important.

First, let's dream a bit together and write down anything you'd like to have, be or do. Don't worry about the timing or whether or not it's truly feasible, just let go a little bit and think about the possibilities. If it's helpful, grab a cup of tea and put on some music for at least ten minutes.

Have (*ie: a beautiful garden*):

_____

_____

_____

_____

_____

_____

_____

Be (*a top earner in my company*):

_____

_____

_____

_____

_____

_____

_____

Do (*travel to Italy with my hubby*):

See? Doesn't that feel fantastic! You can always add to this list as you go along and I like to capture my ideas in a journal I keep with me at all times.

Now we're going to get a bit more specific in each area of your life. For each section, I want you to fill in what you want in present tense affirmation-style statements, using as many descriptive words as possible. Then we'll flesh out the details as the clearer we can get, the easier it is for your subconscious mind to get to work in making it happen!

Here are my suggested categories but feel free to change them as you see fit:
- o Family
- o Faith
- o Financial
- o Health/Fitness
- o Emotional/Self-Development
- o Your Business
- o Leadership Development
- o Friends
- o Relaxation/Hobbies

Example:

Family: I take my children to school every day and love to take my time in the morning and not rush them out the door. On Wednesdays, I always pick them up early and take them to the Farmers Market. We always have such a great time and I love seeing them enjoying real food and understanding where it comes from! I make healthy meals for dinner and surprisingly everyone is always asking for seconds – it's pretty unbelievable😊. It makes me so happy to have dinner around the table as a family and find out how everyone's day was. I'm so thankful for all of the traditions we have as a family and for all of the memories we're creating. I love being a mom!

Purpose: I want to be in my girls' lives as much as possible because I know they will grow up so fast. I believe it is super valuable to create a home life where our family truly enjoys being together and feels secure, safe and loved. And let's face it, moms are the glue that hold it all together!

Power Statement: I'm a Rockstar Mompreneur!

One Year Goal: To be working from home 100%.

Quarterly Goal: To scale back my hours at work to part time.

Action Step: Review finances with my hubby and schedule a meeting with my boss.

Your Turn!

Category:

_____

_____

_____

_____

_____

_____

_____

_____

Purpose:

_____

_____

_____

Power Statement:

_____

_____

_____

One Year Goal:

_____

_____

_____

Quarterly Goal:

_____

_____

_____

Action Step:

....

....

....

....

Chapter 1 Action Steps:

- ❏ Write down your "why" for building your business and refer to it daily. *Date completed:* _____

- ❏ Choose 10-30 things you'd like to have, be or do and write them down in your journal. *Date completed:* _____

- ❏ Complete the goal setting section for at least one area of your life such as faith,

financial, family, fitness, etc. *Date
completed:* _____

CHAPTER 2

Turning Your Dreams into Reality

"Make your life a masterpiece; imagine no limitations on what you can be, have or do."
~Brian Tracy

My absolute favorite way to turn my dreams into reality is by creating vision boards, books, collages or movies. Take a variety of old photos that you love (Facebook is a great place to look) along with images from Google and pick the ones that reflect what you'd like to attract into your life. If losing weight is a goal, you might choose a photo of yourself when you felt healthiest. This can take some time so I do recommend that you schedule an hour or two of uninterrupted time to put together your dreams visually. Choose whichever method you prefer to capture your images but try to put it in a place you'll see daily. Add to it whenever you think of something new!

Breaking through Old Beliefs

Goals are awesome but according to Gay Hendricks in *The Big Leap*, we have to recognize what he calls our upper limits. Upper limits are basically old belief systems that tend to hold us back from growing or reaching new successes in our lives if we don't acknowledge them and work through reframing them. This is especially true when it comes to our association with money because it is so deeply rooted in our family and society as a whole. If you grew up hearing, "*Money doesn't grow on trees,*" you know exactly what I'm talking about.

To help you get started at identifying and reframing your old beliefs, I've picked a few of the most common areas to look at but obviously you'll know what you need to work on most. In the left column, write out your old belief and in the right column create your new belief statement. I've included a ton of affirmation statements to choose from for inspiration but feel free to create your own!

Categories:

- o Money
- o Self-Image
- o Time
- o Ability
- o Health
- o Family
- o Influence/Leadership
- o Running a Business

Affirmation Statements

I have enough money to live comfortably and give abundantly.

Gratitude is the quickest way to abundance.

I live in a rich and prosperous universe.

Money flows to me easily and effortlessly.

I am a money magnet.

I attract runners onto my team.

My team is growing so quickly.

I am a confident closer.

I have prospects coming to *me*.

My bank account is growing more and more every day.

I am highly motivated and productive.

I am hyper focused on my goals and am accomplishing one after the other.

The confidence needed to succeed is within me.

I love myself just the way I am.

I am open to the riches of the universe.

I am getting better and better each and every day.

I have accomplished amazing things.

I feel prosperous at all times.

I attract one opportunity after the other.

I am too blessed to be stressed.

I love, honor and accept myself.

I am amazing.

I am worthy.

I am enough.

Example:

Old Belief	*New Belief*
Money has always been a struggle for me.	Money is abundant and there is plenty for me & everyone else.

List any and all that you can think of here:

Old Belief   *New Belief*

_____   _____

_____   _____

_____   _____

_____   _____

_____   _____

_____   _____

_____   _____

_____   _____

_____   _____

_____   _____

_____   _____

Chapter 2 Action Steps:

❑ Put together either a vision board, book
or movie and try to look at it daily. *Date
completed:* _____

❑ Replace at least three old, limiting beliefs
with new affirmation-style statements.
Date completed: _____

❑ Optional: Create a powerful affirmation statement and print it out and put in a cute frame or have it pop up as a calendar reminder throughout the day. You don't have to stop at one!

CHAPTER 3

Putting Together Your Business Plan

"The quality of a man's life is in direct proportion to his commitment to excellence, whatever his chosen field or endeavor."

~Vince Lombardi

At a minimum, I have my team plan out their goals for the month, but if you can get to a place in your business where you're planning out quarterly or even yearly, that is the sweet spot. Not only does it help you to stay on track, it also allows you to see the big picture of how you're going to achieve the high ranks within your company and how big your team will grow. Don't overthink it and make sure the numbers you put down are a bit uncomfortable yet still exciting.

Sales Goals

Depending on the time of year it is when you're reading this, go to that month and fill these numbers out for 12 months. Think about what you'd like to accomplish a year from now and then work backwards. You can always adjust these numbers as you go along so just do it and don't try to be perfect.

January
Rank: _____

Team Sales: _____

 # in Downline: _____

Income: _____

February
Rank: _____

Team Sales: _____

 # in Downline: _____

Income: _____

March
Rank: _____

Team Sales: _____

 # in Downline: _____

Income: _____

April

Rank: _____

Team Sales: _____

 # in Downline: _____

Income: _____

May

Rank: _____

Team Sales: _____

 # in Downline: _____

Income: _____

June

Rank: _____

Team Sales: _____

 # in Downline: _____

Income: _____

July

Rank: _____

Team Sales: _____

 # in Downline: _____

Income: _____

August

Rank: _____

Team Sales: _____

 # in Downline: _____

Income: _____

September

Rank: _____

Team Sales: _____

 # in Downline: _____

Income: _____

October

Rank: _____

Team Sales: _____

 # in Downline: _____

Income: _____

November

Rank: _____

Team Sales: _____

 # in Downline: _____

Income: _____

December

Rank: _____

Team Sales: _____

 # in Downline: _____

Income: _____

Prospecting Goals

Have you ever wondered what it takes to recruit a certain number of team members each month? This is how you're going to figure this out. Decide what you'd like to set as your monthly goals for prospecting by completing this chart. And to clarify, exposures means how many prospects have agreed to take a look at your opportunity.

	# Exposures	# Customers	#Business Builders
Jan			
Feb			
Mar			
Apr			
May			
Jun			
Jul			
Aug			
Sep			
Oct			
Nov			
Dec			

Decluttering Project

I remember one of the first online coaching programs I did and the first week's homework assignment was to declutter. I was thinking, "*I just paid a bunch of money to...organize?!*" But once I went through the process and started to understand why it was so important, I now implement this same strategy with all of my programs too.

When your environment is cluttered, whether it be physical objects in your home, an inbox full of emails or even computer files that are not organized and easily accessible, it causes clutter and a messy mind. And on top of that, it makes it very difficult to allow good things to come into our lives because there isn't any room for them mentally.

So for this project, I want you to pick one physical area and one digital area to organize. Schedule it right onto your calendar in pen and put some relaxing music on and embrace the activity. Pick areas that you spend the most time in or you notice tend to bother you quite a bit.

Do your best to make them as organized as possible but also be thinking about a way to maintain it. For example, in your office, you could make a rule that any new paper that makes its way into your office has to be filed or placed in your inbox to be tackled right away.

If you want additional resources, my absolute favorite book is called *Organizing from the Inside Out*. Yes, it's super old school but it's legit!

Chapter 3 Action Steps:

- ☐ Fill out the Business Planning section for the remainder of the year. *Date completed:* _____

- ☐ Set up your prospecting goals for the next three months. *Date completed:* _____

- ☐ Declutter an area of your choice and post the before and afters on social media or inside of our group. *Date completed:* _____

- ☐ Optional: Write out a check to yourself with the amount you want to make monthly for your first income goal. Put it somewhere you can see it daily.

- ☐ On-going: And don't forget your daily mindset work implementing journaling, reviewing your vision board, meditating and reading educational books!

CHAPTER 4

Additional Resources Along the Way

"The more that you read, the more things you will know. The more that you learn, the more places you'll go." ~Dr. Seuss

Let's face it, leaders are readers, and constantly growing and improving is the name of the game. Whether it be by holding a good old-fashioned paperback in your hand or listening to a book from Audible, digesting content on a continual basis is so important for your long-term success. Here are my favorites and I will definitely be adding to it as I discover new books!

My 2018 Recommended Reading List

- *You are a Badass*
- *Get Over Your Damn Self*
- *Go Pro*
- *Girl, Wash Your Face*
- *The Game of Network Marketing*
- *Freakishly Effective Social Media for Network Marketers*

- *Get Rich Lucky Bitch*
- *You Can be Awesome*
- *The Barefoot Executive*
- *Miracle Morning for Network Marketers*
- *The 4 Color Personalities of MLM*
- *Go for No*
- *Grit*
- *The Subtle Art of Not Giving a F&$@*
- *Beach Money*
- *How to Make Shit Happen*
- *The Art of Exceptional Living*
- *How to Build Network Marketing Leaders*
- *How I Raised Myself from Failure to Success in Selling*
- *How to Rock Your Network Marketing Business*
- *Flip Flop CEO*
- *The Big Leap*
- *Crush It*
- *The Success Principles*
- *Awaken the Giant Within*
- *The Total Money Makeover*
- *Instagram Secrets*
- *The Four Agreements*

Chapter 4 Action Step:

☐ Choose a book from the list and read the first chapter. *Date completed:*

_____

☐ On-going: And don't forget your daily mindset work implementing journaling, reviewing your vision board, meditating and reading educational books!

CHAPTER 5

Ready, Set, Launch!

"Things do not happen. Things are made to happen." ~John F. Kennedy

I believe in my heart that it's crucial for anyone looking to build a long-term business to take the time to set their goals and work through old belief systems so they can allow themselves to grow and flourish with this new chapter in their life. But just as importantly, it's time to take action! Just like you wouldn't get in your car on a family road trip without a map or your GPS set to go, you don't want to start your business without a plan.

It's a delicate balance but you want to simultaneously be learning how to launch your business while actually taking action. Too many times people get caught up in wanting to watch all the training videos, memorize all the product ingredients and learn all the scripts before they reach out to a single person. Don't let that be you or anyone on your team! Education constipation is a real thing (*yes, I know, I just really did say that*) and it can really hold you back from a solid launch.

Utilize my *The Goal Digger Girl's Getting Started Guide* found in the book resources at thegoaldiggergirl.com/trainings/book-resources/ on my site (*password is rockyourbiz*) anytime you want to launch or relaunch your business and with every single new person you bring onto your team. Implement this with your current team if you've already been with your company for a bit and teach your leaders to do it with their team.

The secret to turning one into thousands (*see Rob Sperry's book at RobSperry.com/blueprint for more details*) is the power of duplication. Too many times we bring a team member on board expecting them to be like us and just run with this business. Unfortunately, it doesn't work like that and the fact of the matter is most people aren't like you and I know this because you're reading this book. So to help you duplicate, let's work through the guide *now* so you have a good grasp of what it covers and are prepared to use it with your next recruit.

Getting Started Guide!

You may or may not remember this but when you were approached about joining this business, you wondered to yourself if you could do it. Remember, your prospects always ask themselves the same thing and that's why it's super important to create simple systems that they can follow and duplicate for their team.

Follow this guide to launch or relaunch your business at any time and do the same for your team for Rockstar results!

Your Why

In a couple of sentences, write down why you joined this business. Did you want more time freedom, extra income or just something to call your own? Whatever it is, it should make your heart feel good and put a smile on your face.

Instead of just writing out the facts, put meaning behind it such as *"I want to be able to drop my girls off at school every day and pick them up so that I can see them as much as possible while they are still young and growing so fast. I don't want to miss anything! I want to bring in enough extra income each month so that I don't feel the burden of our debt on my shoulders and can sleep soundly at night. A romantic vacation away would be nice too!"*

Write your why:

_____

_____

_____

_____

_____

_____

_____

_____

How much money do you want to make? Monthly? In six months? A year from now?

_____

_____

_____

_____

How much time can you commit to daily to work this business? Weekly?

_____

_____

_____

What will you **need to sacrifice** for now to make this happen?

_____

_____

_____

_____

This is network marketing and the success and results don't happen overnight. There *will* be ups and downs. Do you **give your upline permission** to hold you accountable?

_____

Start your Contact List of 100-200 names (*don't prejudge!*) and write them down with pen and paper. It's completely normal to have apprehension around this activity but remember that if no one knows you're in business, you're not in business. Your list is literally your ATM money maker and I'll teach you how to share in a non-spammy, genuine way. Here are some memory joggers to get you started:

*Family
*Besties
*Neighbors
*Co-Workers
*Other Parents
*People at the Gym
*Facebook Friends
*Instagram Followers
*LinkedIn Connections
*Cell Phone Contacts

*Email Address Book

*Teachers at School

*High School Classmates

*College Buddies

*Old-Coworkers

*Other Club Members (*ie: book club*)

*Old Neighbors

*Service People (*ie: stylist, housekeeper, mailman, coffee barista, gardener, doctor, tax advisor, finance person, babysitter, realtor, car salesman, dentist, photographer, etc.*)

Stop and make your list of 100 now ☺.

Schedule your business launch event (*in-person, online, raffle campaign, VIP group*) and coordinate with your upline, ideally within two to three weeks:

_____

_____

_____

_____

Review any **newbie bonuses** available and map out how to get to your **first rank**:

_____

_____

_____

_____

....

Stop here and call your upline to go over this with
you and answer any questions you have (ideally
within 48 hours)!

Putting it Into Action

Step 1: The Text Blitz

Start with the top 25 people closest to you and
send out the text script below. Believe it or not,
the people you think you're going to sign up
right away or buy from possibly aren't so let's
get them out of the way. Most people have to
hear about your product or business a few
times before saying yes so just know it's part of
the process.

Stop and do this right now and let your upline
know when you're done. They can help you with
what to say to the responses you receive.

Script: *"Hey, girl! How are you doing? I am getting the word out to my friends and family in case they know of anyone that could benefit from what I have to offer. I'm launching a new business! I know it's probably not a fit for you and that's totally okay. I would really appreciate it if you shared my information with anyone that might complain about (insert pain point such as weight gain, sensitive skin, hair loss, etc.) for any reason or if someone needs a second stream of income. I would love to help them! I'm super excited and I appreciate your support😊. Here are some before and afters as well. Would you be open to learning more?"*

Step 2: The Curiosity Post
One of the biggest mistakes new business partners make is spamming the newsfeed on Facebook because they're so excited about their new business venture and want the world to know. There are a couple of problems with this approach. Since it's all about you and not them, it can come across as a major turn off for some; especially if they've had a bad experience with

network marketing in the past. Also, since all of the info is just thrown into their lap, it doesn't grab their attention in any way and gives them the upper hand. Here is where we insert the Curiosity Post.

Choose a before and after of your choice and write a compelling description with the intention of engaging your followers to comment on the post. Ask your upline for examples. It's extremely important not to mention the company name or they might go and Google it and that doesn't always go over well. Post no more than one to two times per week unless it's inside a closed Facebook group for your prospects and customers. Here are some examples:

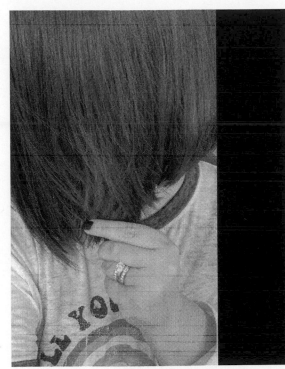

So, I am a week in with the new hair care! Still in love!! I am sure there will be a Black Friday deal on these products. Comment below if you want the details when I find out about them!!

👍 Like   💬 Comment   ➦ Share

⭕⭕ 14

View 5 more comments

Kristi Dully Kimberly Olson, will you let us all know the Black Friday Deal when you find out about it?

Like · Reply · 14w   ⭕ 1

↪ Kimberly Olson replied · 9 Replies

Misty DeRiggi Love their products! Dave does too 😊

Love · Reply · 14w   ⭕⭕ 2

↪ Kimberly Olson replied · 3 Replies

Jackie Elswick Spraker I would love to try it. I have naturally curly hair so I need something to hold the curl and reduce frizz. Does this work for that?

Pamela Moore
August 11 at 6:08 PM · 🌐   •••

I was asked to locate a photo before I started raw, plant-based nutrition into my daily diet & then one after this change over a course of a few months. Here ya go! 😄 Wow! Left pic puffy & boy I look tired lol! 😴 Right pic less puffy & of course after shedding 11 lbs & better sleep! 😌 Bonus point. I do have salon hair lol! 💇 Much more work to do...but I'm healing from the inside out! 💜 OFF my BP meds after 2 years of being on Lisinopril. AMEN to that!! 🙏 I'm loving every min of this journey! 😊
Thank you Dr Dana McGrady for sharing that first $50 gift card with me! #Lifer 💜

Step 3: The Facebook Live

If reading that makes your stomach turn, don't panic and stick with me here. It is highly recommended that you incorporate Facebook Lives into your social media activity, but it is not required. However, keep in mind that people buy from those that they know, like and trust and I believe Facebook Lives are hands down the best way to get your message out to your followers.

When you're ready, you can do your first Facebook Live sharing why you decided to join your company, a product unboxing, or a review of some of the products and why they're awesome. Don't post your link anywhere but rather share the info one-on-one in Facebook messenger.

Daily Activity

Those that are successful in network marketing are the ones that work at their business every single day. This is network marketing, not netwish marketing, so know that to truly achieve the success you want, you have to work at it daily. A good guideline is to share your product or business with two new people a day, five days a week. Find ways to meet new people online and offline constantly and add them to your contact list. Be organized with your list so that you remember to follow up with them because as Eric Worre says in *Go Pro*, "the fortune is in the follow up."

In Closing

Because this is such an emotional business, there will be times when you wonder if you can do this or if you are good enough. I can tell you without even knowing you that you are absolutely 100% good enough and can do this business. There is a huge learning curve, however, the blessing is that you can earn while you learn. Just know that all the work you are doing today will pay off and it will be so worth the reward, you will wonder why you waited this long to jump into network marketing.

You have something special to offer and that's you. Be excited about your product, stand behind your company, but most importantly, believe in yourself. You have a chance to make this business whatever you want it to be, so what are you waiting for? Go out there and let the world know what you're all about!

Chapter 5 Action Steps:

- ❏ Decide a short-term monthly income goal to start and write down how much you want to be making per month a year from now. *Date completed:* _____

- ❏ Add at least 100-200 names to your contact list. *Date completed:*

  _____

- ❏ Do a text blitz where you text or message 25 people. *Date completed:*

  _____

❑ Do a product-related curiosity post using the examples in this book. *Date completed:* _____

❑ Identify which opportunity video you will share when someone is open to taking a look at what you have to offer. *Date completed:* _____

❑ On-going: And don't forget your daily mindset work implementing journaling, reviewing your vision board, meditating and reading educational books!

CHAPTER 6

Your Follow Up System

"Diligent follow up and follow through will set you apart from the crowd and communicate excellence."
~John C. Maxwell

Well here we are just cruising along and ready to tackle organization. If you're not moving through the content as quickly as you'd hoped, implement the time blocking method in the next chapter's materials and schedule it in. We make the time for what is most important to us, and I know this is a top priority for you as you've already invested time and money into this book.

You may feel very "busy" throughout the day, but the end results of your productivity are what are most important. You can't determine whether or not a prospect will become a customer or join your team, but you can control how much daily activity you put in. I will teach you what to be doing daily to add prospects to your list, how to track them efficiently and follow up consistently so you can eventually convert them. Organization is the name of the game!

Prospect Management

When I first joined my network marketing company, I reached out to a ton of people via text or on Facebook Messenger. Most responded with some sort of interest so it was my responsibility to follow up with them. There were so many messages here and there that a lot of people fell through the cracks. I quickly realized I needed some sort of system to keep track of everyone and follow up accordingly.

There are three main formats I've seen that work in this industry but of course find what works for you. Here's a brief summary of each and I'd also recommend watching some tutorials on YouTube to learn more about each option.

Paper: with this method, all leads go onto a master list in a notebook. Once they become a prospect (after you've exposed them with your product or company), they are then moved to another section in the notebook for follow up. Customers can be moved to another section as well as business builders that join your team.

The upside to this method is that when we write something down, we make a connection to it in more of a creative way than just typing it. Also, it's nice because you can "see" all of your leads right in front of you at all times. However, it is extremely cumbersome to move your names throughout the different sections, keep track of when to follow up with them and you also lose the ability to sort the list by common denominators such as last follow up date.

Digital Spreadsheets: using programs such as Excel or Smartsheet are a way to capture all your leads digitally but you are in charge of manually tracking them. You can create different columns or even tabs to identify your leads, prospects, customers, and business builders. The way you want to set up the format is completely up to you. Also, an app is available for most systems. If you opt for Excel, download

Google Sheets on your phone so you can keep your notes updated and synced up on the fly.

With Smartsheet you can automate the follow up process by setting reminders that come straight to your email inbox on their due date. Another neat feature is that you can link your contact's name directly to their Facebook page for easy accessibility. Outside of that, you are responsible for keeping up with your list on a daily basis.

Online Programs: there are many online programs available for contact management, but I'll just touch on one as an example as it's specific to network marketing. Teamzy is an online system built by network marketers designed to help you stay organized with your contacts. *(Note: I've heard great things about Hubspot and Asana as well)*.

Since this platform is designed for network marketers, you can fill out some info when setting up your account and it'll tell you how many people you need to "expose" daily to reach your income goals. All of your contacts are imported from Facebook so it is very robust with its options. The one drawback is that you can't see all of your contacts at once so you have to be really diligent about how you label them with tags, etc. to easily retrieve them from the software.

Whichever system you choose, take your initial list that you created with your warm leads and put everyone and their brother on there that you can possibly think of. Go through your cell phone contacts and Facebook friends and add them to your prospect list. You'll want this list to be in the hundreds. Think big! I'll teach you how to add tons of cold leads to this list next and soon we'll go through the process to turn them into a warm prospect.

Chapter 6 Action Steps:
- ❑ Go through all your texts, Facebook messages, notebooks, etc. to gather all your leads and add them to your list. Get

this number to 300+. *Date completed:*

_____

❑ Choose which method you will utilize to keep track of your prospects and add your list to it. Maintain your list for a week straight by following up accordingly. *Date completed:*

_____

❑ On-going: And don't forget your daily mindset work implementing journaling, reviewing your vision board, meditating, and reading educational books!

CHAPTER 7

Crushing Your Daily Activity

"Results always follow activity. Always."
~Kimberly Olson

Daily Method of Operation (DMO)

No matter what system you choose, just like a traditional brick and mortar business, you need a system. And the same goes for your daily method of operation, also known as DMO. If you study the most successful people in the network marketing industry, they have a standard DMO that they follow religiously, day in and day out. And as we've discussed, you can't control the outcome of your activity, but you can control your daily activity.

What is included in your daily activity is up to you based on your goals, but I've put together a tracker to get you started. It is very comprehensive so keep that in mind and tweak it to fit your desired activity. Let's review *The Goal Digger Girl's Daily Activity Tracker* now so you can get a clear picture of what you will want to incorporate on a daily basis (*download at thegoaldiggergirl.com/trainings/book-resources/ and use password rockyourbiz to access it*).

The Goal Digger Girl's Weekly Activity Tracker

Morning	Monday	Tuesday	Wednesday	Thursday	Friday	Saturday	Sunday
Post on Facebook (personal/groups)							
Post on Facebook Stories							
Post on Instagram and in IG Stories/Check Comments							
Check Messenger							
Check Notifications							
Comment on People's Posts who Comment on My Posts							
Add 10 New Friends (delete as needed)							
Send Happy Birthday Messages							
Comment on 10 Posts from See 1st Friends							
Mid-Day							
Post on Facebook (personal/groups)							
Check Messenger							
Check Notifications							
Evening							
Facebook Live 2-3 times Weekly (personal/groups)							
Check Messenger							
Check Notifications							
Comment on People's Posts who Comment on My Posts							
Add 10 New Friends (delete as needed)							
Add Value to 1-3 Private Groups (ie: NM Moms)							
Comment on 10 Posts from See 1st Friends							
Daily Totals:							
# of New Exposures (product or business opportunity)							
# of New Customers							
# of New Business Partners							
Weekly Total:							

Types of Posts: inspiring, empowering, personal share, product post, biz post, entertaining, educational/tips, lives

Time Blocking

The thought of that much activity several times a day can be overwhelming for some so I want to teach you time blocking and how to be intentional on Facebook. Go onto Facebook (*or any other social media platform*) with a plan, otherwise you'll get sucked into the newsfeed and be wasting a *ton* of time. Most of you know how crazy my schedule is and the only way I've been able to be effective and build my businesses while juggling a young family is by time blocking.

Going back to Chapter 1 where you chose the different areas of life that are important to you, you'll want to have those in your sight as you plan out your week and schedule your time blocking. Basically, time blocking is literally scheduling everything you want to accomplish. For example, if one of your goals was to lose weight, you'd want to schedule in your workout times in advance and stick with them as if they were a doctor's appointment.

I like to take time every Sunday to review my goals and then pay attention to how much time I'm spending in each area to be as balanced as possible. Of course, some areas will take more attention than others, but this can help you redirect your efforts rather quickly if you get off track. Because your daily activity is the most important part of your network marketing business, you've got to schedule it in every day.

Delegating

Oh my word, Goal Digger! When I think back to the hours upon hours I spent mailing out samples to prospects, I want to cringe. It made sense to do it myself when I started out, but once my business started growing, it would have made more sense to find someone else who could do it for me. Do you have a teenager who would love to help you super part-time, or a friend? Trading product for services is one of the best old-school ways to get some help on your side without breaking the bank.

To determine if you should delegate the activity or do it yourself, the first question to ask yourself: Is this an IPA (*no, not the beer* 😊 *– an Income Producing Activity*)? If yes, you should be doing it. That is the number one priority of your business and you need to have your hands in it.

If it isn't, then you can determine what your estimated worth is per hour and decide if it makes more sense for you to do it or contract someone else to do it. Just take your monthly income from your business divided by the number of hours you worked to make that and that's your current worth.

I've had the most success using referrals, otherwise try the contracting website called UpWork to hire Virtual Assistants, Web Designers, etc. If you want help on social media with a Facebook group cover or for graphics to post, you can also go to Fiverr for super affordable ways to get these types of jobs done.

Saying No

I know it's super cliché, but honestly, if you really want to make network marketing a career or reach six figures and beyond, you have to get really good at saying no. You need to say no to invitations, commitments, online distractions, Netflix, Real Housewives, etc. I know that sounds extreme, and I get it, but I'm not asking you to do it forever.

A lot of times network marketers get frustrated because they're not seeing the progress in their business that they'd hoped for. But what they don't realize is that often they're working their business way less than they need to in order to make their dreams a reality. Start with saying no to the things that eat away at your productivity and go from there.

Chapter 7 Action Steps:

❑ Print *The Goal Digger Girl's Daily Activity Tracker* and do a three day challenge to complete the list daily (*tweak as needed*).

Do the challenge with your team for even better results! *Date completed:*

_____

☐ With your goals in front of you, take out your planner and schedule everything out down to 30-minute increments for one week. *Date completed:* _____

☐ Practice not saying yes to anyone or anything right away – say you will get back to them. *Date completed:*

_____

☐ On-going: And don't forget your daily mindset work implementing journaling, reviewing your vision board, meditating and reading educational books!

CHAPTER 8

"Build the right relationships with the right people and nurture them over time and you'll always have a leg up on the competition."

~Paul May

Well, Goal Digger, we are just cruising through this book. I've had a ton of positive testimonials flooding in so I'm so pleased that not only are you finding value in the content, but you're implementing it! That's the name of the game. So far, the material has been pretty big picture but now we'll get down into the nitty gritty for the remainder of our time together.

It can be a bit overwhelming when you open up your Facebook app, click the post button, but then sit there and wonder what the heck you should post! There is something so vulnerable about sharing what's on your mind – especially original content. However, once you get the hang of this and learn how to share who you really are and not spam all your friends, you're going to fall in love with the entire process. And a fantastic side effect is a dramatic boost to your visibility on Facebook and other social media platforms as well. So, let's dive in!

Attraction Marketing

This is a term that is now thrown around a lot so let's break it down and look at what it really means. When you think of a brick and mortar business, such as a clothing boutique, think about all the elements involved to draw you in. It would have an appealing sign out front, an attractive display case, friendly and positive employees, and showcase its best throughout the store. Your personal Facebook page is the same thing.

Your profile picture needs to be a clear headshot of yourself – just you, and one that you don't change too often (*this is your store sign*). It can be a selfie or a professional shot but get a nice closeup that is easy to see when others see you in post threads or in Messenger. Your cover image can change more frequently, even weekly, as this is your "display case." I love seeing great family shots, vacation destinations or inspirational quotes.

Remove the name of your company and any links to your company page. If people can click the link and go scope it out on their own, why would they need to build a relationship or see what you're all about? In addition, you run the risk of them Googling your company and the majority of network marketing companies have negative stuff floating around the internet about them. Also, not blasting your company name all over the place is part of the attraction which we'll get into shortly with creating curiosity through our posts.

Clean up any old photos from college or anything this is not falling into the fun *AND* classy category. Even though it's your personal page, we want it set on public to get you the biggest reach possible so it needs to be professional. In addition, I recommend being more like Switzerland when it comes to your opinions because unfortunately there is a lot of emotion one way or the other and that could turn off a potential customer or business builder.

Most importantly, be thinking of what is attractive to others. This isn't about being somebody you're not, but about "showcasing" your best attributes, just like the boutique owner would do in her store. When prospects visit your profile, you want them to have a good experience and be drawn to or intrigued to learn more about you. That's what attraction marketing is all about.

Content Creation

Download my Content Calendar (*found at thegoaldiggergirl.com/trainings/book- resources/ and the password is rockyourbiz*) and fill it out to plan your content in advance. Start posting twice a day with a variety of non-spammy content such as:

  o Personal (*selfies, your kids, etc*).
  o Inspirational

- Funny/Entertaining
- Opinion
- Educational
- Polls
- Product Posts (*1-2 times a week*)
- Business Posts (*1-2 times a week*)
- Facebook Lives
- Giveaways

Pay attention to what gets engagement and tweak future posting based off of that. As soon as you post, Facebook's algorithm decides in about 30 minutes whether or not to show your post to the rest of your friends. Here are some tips:

- Like your post and comment right away to piggyback on what you've already said about the post. Or ask your mom to comment!
- Put a call to action in the post description to encourage engagement.
- Keep an eye on it at first and respond quickly to anyone who comments.

o For anyone who comments, go to their profile and comment on one of their recent posts (*Facebook loves how social this is!*).

o Keep a folder of your highest engaging posts and recycle them every other month or so. Eventually you can draw from Facebook memories for content to repurpose.

o Be consistent with how frequently you're posting or doing Facebook lives. Your audience will begin to follow you and needs to know what to expect from you.

o Use *The Goal Digger Girl's Daily Activity Tracker* to stay organized.

o You can schedule your posts in groups and on pages if that is helpful to you.

o Don't post just to post; think it through😉.

o Be genuine and authentic and you can't go wrong!

Facebook Stories

As I write this, there is so much changing with Facebook Stories that I guarantee you this will become an extremely relevant part of your business compared to where it stands today. I was just reading how Instagram Stories are being viewed *triple* the amount of the posts shown in the newsfeed. That's leverage. Also, Facebook loves it when you use all of its various features and will favor you within the algorithm when you venture into Facebook Stories.

When you think of Facebook Stories, I want you to the think about being behind the scenes of a movie set. You know how neat it is to see what it really takes to create a movie or what actors and actresses have to do to make it all happen? It's the same thing with Facebook Stories. You want to give your followers a glimpse into your day to day activity, as much as four different posts a day. Maybe you share a sweaty selfie in the morning, an awesome new smoothie recipe you've tried for the first time and then show a curiosity post about your product later that day.

I'll be honest that just like Facebook Lives, it does take some time to get the hang of what to post and to keep it consistent with what you're posting on your personal page. But if you're diligent with the process, consistent, and willing to have some fun, you're going to get *SO* much more exposure and a ton of new leads. We'll talk more about what to do with them in the next chapter, but everyone who views your story is a potential lead. And they actively clicked your story to take a look at what's happening in your life, versus reactively seeing what you've posted that comes up in their newsfeed. Powerful.

Facebook Lives

Once I got over my fear of doing Facebook lives, my business completely changed as well as my confidence in myself and what I had to offer. You want to feel incredible? Start getting comfortable with Facebook lives!

At the beginning of 2018, Facebook announced that it's #1 priority will be Facebook lives. Your lives will get you in front of thousands of people instead of maybe a hundred on a strong post. In addition, doing lives gives you instant credibility (*like being on TV*) and can help you to have prospects reach out to YOU.

What to cover in your lives is hands down the question I get most often from people and the answer is so much simpler than you'd think. You can have a theme for your lives (*positivity, mindset, inspiration, wellness*) but honestly to start, just start! Ask your friends what they go to you for, notice what you're best at teaching, do a poll or just learn something new and turn around and teach it. Remember there is always someone you know more than and if you can impact one person, you've done your job.

Whatever you choose, be consistent. Don't go live for five days in a row and then become a ghost for months. Evening times when the kids are in bed is a great time and Facebook is very active at night. You can look inside your Messenger app to see how many of your friends are active at different times of day but honestly do what works for you!

Let's take a look at some titles for ideas but I definitely encourage you to put some thought into them. I always choose my title ahead of time and save it in notepad on my cell so I'm not scrambling right before going live. Use emojis and create curiosity so that people want to know more and hop on to see what your live is all about.

Examples:

⚡️📎What you literally have to do to get people to say YES! This can help you: *know how often to follow up with prospects *know what to say with each exposure *learn how to ask for the sale naturally instead of being spammy Ya ready ?!
...
How to stop prospecting and start recruiting! Watch this if: *you have someone interested but then hear crickets *you get a conversation going but can't seem to close them *you just want to enjoy the whole process more!
...

Want to know how to have "posture" on social media so you can attract a huge tribe and become a confident closer 🔍? Then tune in now!

...

How to grow your team Sales with Taprooting ⚡ ✴ 💬 📎 and the power of Duplication!

...

Jot down topic ideas here and keep a running list as ideas come to you:

_____

_____

_____

_____

_____

_____

_____

Other Tips

- o Have notes prepared because this will keep you on point and prevent you from "squirreling" or rambling. Include your intro (*name/live topic*), your experience with the topic, 3-5 tips, then finish with a call to action.

- Find a designated place that is quiet where you can do your lives. Have a non-distracting background and good lighting.
- Go live on your phone or iPad versus a computer. Get comfortable with the filters (*you can choose to go live to yourself to practice*).
- Avoid tagging people in the title unless appropriate; instead do it in the comments. Also, don't put links in the title.
- Drive up engagement by saying, "*put 1 in the comments if you're watching this live, 2 if you're on the replay,*" etc. Most are replay viewers so don't wait for people to get on when you go live.
- The length of time depends on the content – mine average 15 to 18 minutes but you can get great content out in less than 10.
- Respond to every single comment after you're done because that will drive up the algorithm and get you in front of more people!

- Think long-term with these and remember the goal is to become an influencer. You want to gain their trust, share your journey and let them get to know who you are and what you have to offer.
- Focus on helping and teaching, not on the number of views.
- Embrace #ProgressNotPerfection

Chapter 8 Action Steps

❑ Update your profile picture and bio section to remove the company name and implement the attraction marketing principles discussed. *Date completed:*

_____

❑ Plan out your posts with my *Social Media Content Calendar* and fill it out completely. *Date completed:*

_____

❑ Tweak your post descriptions to implement call-to-actions until you start to get increasing engagement on your posts. *Date completed:* _____

❑ Brainstorm Facebook Live topics and write down at least ten ideas. *Date completed:* _____

❑ Using the ideas in this book, write down several title starters that you can expand on for a variety of Lives. *Date completed:* _____

❑ Come up with a weekly Facebook Live series that has a theme and try to be consistent with day and time. *Date completed:* _____

❑ Do a Facebook Live (*take a deep breath; you've got this!*). *Date completed:* _____

❏ On-going: And don't forget your daily mindset work implementing journaling, reviewing your vision board, meditating and reading educational books!

CHAPTER 9

Passionate Prospecting

"Getting to know someone else involves curiosity about where they have come from, who they are." ~Penelope Lively

The question I get most often from my audience is how to recruit people online. There is a lot of bad information out there, confusion and straight up anxiety around the whole topic. So hang in there and not only will I show you how to do it the right way (*in my opinion*), I will show you how to enjoy the entire process and actually look forward to your next interaction. And remember, your opportunity is a potential blessing to others and we're not in the business of convincing people☺.

Posture

When you're connecting with potential customers and business builders, it's extremely important that you practice coming from a place of abundance instead of lack. People will absolutely respond differently to you based on your mindset.

Take control of the conversation, have confidence in yourself and be an authority in the situation. You want to be seen as a leader. Even if you have to fake it until you make it, that is how you will need to go about it for now.

I recommend incorporating daily mindset practices where you visualize people saying yes, your team growing quickly, and for you to open up your inbox and it's full of prospects saying they want to know more! It may seem silly, but it absolutely works. And really what do you have to lose?

Starting the Conversation

I'm going to assume you've already worked through your warm market and if you haven't already, exhaust that list first before moving onto cold leads. Cold leads cannot be prospected until they've become warm, so you'll almost always be at an advantage working through true warm leads before moving onto your cold market.

When it comes to cold leads, the best ones to prospect are the ones that proactively interact with you and open up the door to a conversation. This will come in various ways such as someone sending you a friend request, watching your Facebook story or commenting/liking/reacting to your posts. Even better are those that share your posts!

If they send you a friend request, message them back and say something such as, *"Thanks for the friend request – I love connecting with new people on Facebook. I saw your adorable girls – I have two as well. How old are they?"* Continue getting to know them until you can find a pain point and bring up your business opportunity or product. We'll cover exactly what to say in a bit.

If they interacted with one of your posts or Facebook stories, you can message them and say, *"Hey, there! I saw (insert whatever action they took) that you watched my Facebook live, what was your favorite part?"* Remember you're the expert, so look for opportunities to mentor them since they were proactively digesting your content.

Request 10-20 new friends a day and add them to your prospect list. Look for people who fit your ideal team member or customer and always scope out their profile before adding. Create a section on your prospecting list to keep track of how often you interact with their page. You will want to comment on there a few times before taking the conversation to messenger. Get to know them! Pay attention to what they're posting to find out more about them but also to hopefully find out their pain points.

One of my favorite places to connect with like-minded people are in Facebook groups. If you're patient, you can actually develop some amazing connections inside of these groups. I'd focus on no more than three at a time that way you can keep up with it and add value when appropriate. Don't spam the group or ever share your company name, product or link.

Look for ways to add value in an authentic way. If someone interacts with your comment or post, they are a lead (*same as the above mentioned*). If they comment on a post in the group and you really like what they've contributed, you can reach out to them via messenger and tell them that. *"Hey, there! I'm also in Eric Worre's group and I loved what you said about trading time for money – how long have you been an entrepreneur?"*

The reason why I love sending birthday messages (*voice is optimal*), is because not many do it but also because it's a great way to connect with every single person on your friends list. If they don't respond back, I delete them. If they do, I connect with them, build rapport and look for a way to share what I have to offer.

The last one I like to cover is cold leads you meet in person. A solid tip from the book *Go Pro* is to always be in a hurry when conversing with a prospect in person. Compliment them and say, *"I should really tell you what I do!"* Then get their number or connect on Facebook and go from there.

Other ways are to ask for referrals if someone you approach isn't interested at the moment. Or you can ask one of your current customers to host an online party and invite all their friends. My favorite way is to share my company's referral program with current customers and ask who they know that could also benefit from the product or business. You just never know!

What to Say

Here are some Do's and Don'ts before we get into exactly what to say to prospects:

- o Don't ever copy and paste a script. Facebook knows you're doing it, your prospects know you're doing it and you know you're doing it. It's a lose-lose all around. I'd rather you read a script on voice messenger if you're that unsure of what to say.

- o Never become defensive or rude if they're not interested or respond negatively.
- o Find their pain point and tweak your story accordingly.
- o Use voice messenger whenever possible.
- o When you're new, work towards a three-way group chat or call so your upline can assist you.
- o Use 3rd party validation tools such as videos, testimonials, PDFs or private Facebook groups.
- o Don't prospect everyone – be selective about who you're recruiting and think long-term.

Samples Scripts for Success

Intro to Warm Market (*leading with product*)

"Hey, girl! How are you doing? I am getting the word out to my friends and family in case they know of anyone that could benefit from what I have to offer. I'm launching a new business! I know it's probably not a fit for you and that's

totally okay. I would really appreciate it if you shared my information with anyone that might complain about (insert pain point such as weight gain, sensitive skin, hair loss, etc.) for any reason or if someone needs a second stream of income. I would love to help them! I'm super excited and I appreciate your support 😊. *Here are some before and after's as well. Would you be open to learning more?"*

Intro to Warm Market (*leading with business*)

"I wanted to see if we could hop on the phone to chat about what I'm doing. I promise I won't waste your time. It may or may not be a fit for you, but would you be open to hearing more?"

They said YES to Learning More

"Awesome. I'll tag you in a short video with more info. When you're done watching it, you're going to have questions so I'll introduce you to my amazing friend Kimberly. She's awesome and knows so much about the business. So, we're gonna talk to her after you've watched it so let

me know when you're done." Then put them in a group chat/call with your upline (if possible), otherwise follow up one-on-one. Bonus option – use the reminder feature in Facebook messenger for your follow up time.

Asking your Cold Market

Reminder, never send this to someone you haven't gotten to know first. You should at least be able to have an idea of what their pain point is or how your opportunity could add value to their life or offer a solution.

"Based on what you've shared with me, I think you might want to take a look at what I do. It may or may not be a fit for you, but would you be open to learning more?"

The Scale from 1 to 10 Close

When the opportunity is right during a chat in messenger or on the phone, you're going to want to ask them if they'd like to get started. Statistics show that many people do not buy the first time they're asked, so the majority of your prospects will say no. You can follow up with this:

"On a scale from 1 to 10, 1 being I'm not ready at all to a 10 being I'm in, where are you at?" [Let them pick a number] *"Okay, what would it take to get you to a 10?"*

Objections

Money

"I completely understand. I felt the same way actually but what I found is most people are able to sell something, borrow it or make some quick cash if it's important enough to them. Can I help you brainstorm a plan?"

If they seem eager to try to find the money, work with them on it. Otherwise it's most likely just an excuse.

Time

"I hear you – I was working a full-time job raising two toddlers when I started, but that is exactly why you need this business in your life. Now I have time freedom and a flexible schedule. If I showed you how to work this business into the

nooks and crannies of your day, would you be in?"

Wants to Think About It

This is usually an excuse or they just don't want to flat out tell you they're not interested. Remember, it's not a no, it's just not right now. It takes multiple exposures for the average prospect.

"Sure thing, I totally get it. Do you just need some time to make a decision or is there any other information you need to make that happen?"

I'm Not Good at Sales

"Good! This is not about selling someone or being pushy, it's just about sharing something you're excited about. If I could show you how we use the social sharing method without being annoying or spammy, would that change things for you?"

I've done MLM Before

"I actually said no too because I wasn't successful before. I would just think about the

fact that not all companies and products are the same. Network marketing is so different now too – not bothering your friends and family. And just think about what if you did jump in and it actually worked for you?"

Crafting Your Story

This can take some time to get the hang of, but you'll want to craft your unique story. Ideally, it's less than 60 seconds in length that way you can keep people's attention easily. Also, try to tweak it based on the prospect's background/situation/pain points. Here's an example of mine:

I'm a busy mom with two toddlers and I'd been working full time and running a couple of businesses nights and weekends to make ends meet. Because I was working so much, I missed Elise's first steps and began looking for a way to be home more but still make a great income. My friend introduced me to the company I am with now. She'd completely replaced her income from her full-time job and was driving a nice SUV around that she earned through her company. I quickly realized this would be the way for me to make my transition to working from home. Since then I've grown a team of almost a thousand, become completely debt free and now have a very flexible schedule that I love. And I get to teach others to do the same!

When it comes to your story, don't force working it into the conversation or feel like you have to rehearse it and rattle it off whenever you can. But you'll want to really work on bringing emotion into the conversation. This makes you relatable and also can trigger something in your prospects to get them to start seeing what your opportunity can do for them.

The Fortune is in the Follow Up

One of the biggest mistakes newbie network marketers make is not following up. When someone says no, not interested or goes silent, they take it personally and become fearful about reaching back out. What they don't know is that most people are just busy and forget to respond back or are just not ready right now. Psychologically, people need to be *"exposed"* many, many times before saying yes to anything.

Which one do you want to be?
48% of people NEVER follow up with a new prospect
25% of people make a second contact and stop
12% of people only make three contacts and stop
ONLY 10% make more than three contacts
2% of sales are made on the first contact
3% of sales are made on the second contact
5% of sales are made on the third contact
10% of sales are made on the fourth contact
80% of sales are made on the fifth to twelfth contact

As Eric Worre says in the book *Go Pro*, *"The fortune is in the follow up."* You'll want to come up with a creative way to follow up. Examples are to follow up on a video you sent them, a sample, a PDF document, a flash sale, an event, a new product, or offering the business opportunity if you lead with the product or vice versa, etc. Whatever you choose to follow up with, schedule your next follow up immediately or you will forget!

Chapter 9 Action Steps:

- ❏ Request 10-20 new friends daily following the instructions in the module. *Date completed:* _____

- ❏ Write out your "story" following the process described in this chapter. D*ate completed:* _____

- ❏ Join three new Facebook groups and pop in daily to engage and see who you can connect with. *Date completed:*

  _____

- ❏ Choose from the various ways I shared on finding new people to connect with and reach out to ten new people a day for five days this week. *Date completed:*

  _____

❑ Take out your original list and reach back out to at least twenty people. *Date completed:* _____

❑ On-going: And don't forget your daily mindset work implementing journaling, reviewing your vision board, meditating and reading educational books!

CHAPTER 10

Inspire on Instagram

"Champions are made from something they have deep inside them – a desire, a dream, a vision." ~Muhamid Ali

I don't know about you, but I am pumped to help you get your Instagram on! Whether you want to grow your following, proactively prospect or even become an influencer, I've got you covered. Let's dive in!

Making Instagram Work for YOU

I don't know about you, but I honestly cringe every time I'm scrolling through posts and see other network marketers or entrepreneurs spamming their newsfeed day after day. I think this is often why prospects are hesitant about joining because they think they have to do that to be successful and it couldn't be further from the truth.

Instead of trying to convince people to join your team, why not build up your online presence to a place where prospects are coming to you? It really is the best feeling when you have a conversation and they say, "I've been watching you for a while and I want to know more." Score! That means you're doing your social media the right way.

Just as we discussed in Chapter 8, the same principles apply in regards to cleaning up your profile and making sure it's attractive to visitors. Go ahead and archive any images that aren't aligned with the direction you'd like to go in.

Take the opportunity to update your profile section with a few descriptions that sum up the key attributes you'd like to share about yourself (*see mine for examples at http://instagram.com/TheGoalDiggerGirl*). Set your account to public and add a link directing followers to your private Facebook group or website depending on your targeting. You can switch it to a business account to gain valuable data within the insights feature or download an app such as Iconosquare.

Content Creation Tweaks for Instagram

In addition to the content suggestions already discussed, tie these in to your Instagram as well:

- o Recorded Videos (*1-minute max*)
- o Product Endorsements (*your fav's*)
- o Reposts (use an app such as Regrammer and tag them)

Have a consistent look no matter what you post. Try to choose the same filter within Instagram or try apps such as VSCO or Color Stories. Check out Jenna Kutcher's or Rachel Hollis's for ideas. Every so often, check out your "grid," which is your nine most recent posts. This is what your visitors will see and is the first impression they have of you. Archive anything that doesn't go with the look and feel of what you're all about.

The engagement principles for Instagram are very similar to Facebook with a few variations. As soon as you post, Instagram's algorithm decides in about 10 minutes whether or not to show your post to the rest of your followers. Here are some tips:

- o Utilize an engagement pod. Basically, this is with a group of other Instagrammers and you all commit to liking and commenting every time the others post. It does take some extra work but it is *so* worth it! I set these pods up in all of my Instagram Bootcamps and you can also look inside of Facebook groups to find some to join. Some are free and some have a fee. I recommend you participate in one whether it be with me or a different group.
- o Like your post and comment with a set of hashtags that go along with your post.
- o Keep an eye on it at first and respond quickly to anyone who comments.
- o For anyone who comments, go to their profile and comment on one of their recent posts (*Instagram also loves how social this is!*).

- o Be consistent with how frequently you're posting or doing Instagram lives. Your audience will begin to follow you and needs to know what to expect from you.
- o You can schedule your posts in the Later app or use SecretIGapp.com to even schedule your stories. Avoid third party posting tools as the algorithm is not a fan.

Building up your Followers

Now that you're consistently posting and gaining some momentum with your Instagram page, you're most likely starting to get some new followers. That's extremely exciting and the best part is, this is just the beginning. Just wait until you hit your first 1,000 followers (*if you haven't already*) – it is the *BEST* feeling☺. To make that happen sooner than later, let's start following to gain new followers!

Buying Followers

One tempting strategy to building up your following quickly is to buy followers. With websites such as Fiverr in your face, it can seem like the way to go. However, Instagram has a very sophisticated algorithm and you run the risk of getting your account shut down or at the very least to be put into Instagram jail. Also, if followers are inactive for a certain period of time, Instagram will automatically cause them to unfollow you after a while so it will only serve you in the short term anyway.

Aggressively Following Others in a Safe Manner

The method that has worked for me to build up my following relatively quickly is to manually and consistently, day in and day out, follow other accounts. It takes a ton of time and you have to be really committed to the process, but it really is worth it. You can also make a game out of it to see how many new followers you can attract daily. Please keep in mind Instagram can change its perimeters at any time but this is the most accurate info at this time.

You'll want to find other accounts that are in your niche or something that compliments it. If you're in network marketing, other success-minded, motivational, entrepreneurial-type accounts would be a great fit. Find a good account and click on their followers. Go through and check the profile image and name and make sure they look like someone you'd want to follow. *Do not* scroll down and follow as many as you can, as fast as you can. That will flag Instagram and get you into trouble. Instead, follow no more than 50 an hour and go through them organically, not quickly like a bot.

Once I got my account to where I was following several hundred people, I started unfollowing people as I was adding new accounts to follow. You don't want to be following way more people than are following you. Also note that the max you can follow is 7,500. My favorite app for this is Cleaner for IG but there are many other choices out there.

I also recommend sharing your Instagram posts to Facebook. If they're not linked, simply share the URL to your personal page (*you may have to upload the original image first*) and say at the bottom of your post description: To see more posts like this, follow me on Instagram @TheGoalDiggerGirl! You can also share your Instagram URL to your page or group and call it #FridayFollow where you encourage everyone to follow each other's accounts.

Hashtag #Hashtag

It's time to tackle the elusive topic of hashtags. Yes, they are important. They can help potential followers find you that wouldn't have otherwise. If you can rank up in the top of certain hashtag categories, it can help you to become viewed as an influencer. You can also use them specifically to promote contests, giveaways, raffles, campaigns – you name it. Always search it first to see how competitive the space is for that specific hashtag.

The max number of hashtags to use per post is 30. I like to bury mine in the comments so my posts look cleaner from the start. Try to change them up and have some relevant ones for that specific post each time too. Use the app Leetags for ideas and look at other people's posts to get inspired. I save all of mine in my notepad app on my phone and just pick and choose based on the theme of my post.

Find your best hashtags by posting and then going over to the search field to see if you show up in the top results for that specific hashtag. If it's a super popular hashtag, it doesn't make sense to use it if you're not going to show up in the results, unless it is specifically part of the wording for your post description. Play around with it and save the best ones. Also, throw in geotags (*location-based tags*) once or twice a week as they get up to 79% more engagement than regular posts!

Becoming an Influencer

Even if you're just starting out, you can quickly become an influencer by showing up consistently, offering great content and by interacting with your followers. You want to get to a place where your followers look forward to your next post. You want them to turn on their post notifications and always stop scrolling through the newsfeed when they see your name. The best way to do that is to focus on five topics and rotate through them as you post.

There are three crucial places on Instagram that you can set yourself apart from others. The first part is Instagram Stories. People are watching Stories up to four times more than the newsfeed – which is crazy if you think about it! Shoot for 2-4 posts a day and play around with the different features. The max length of time for video uploads in the Stories section is 15 seconds. Use the app Continual to break your longer video up into 15 seconds and then load them into your Stories in order. Magic!

The second place to really stand out is by doing Instagram Lives. You'll actually go Live inside of your stories and it'll stay up for 24 hours. You do have the option to save it and I highly recommend doing that so you can repurpose it on Facebook whenever you want. For anyone that comments, you can reply back and it goes right into their inbox which is awesome. I love the filters they have too FYI.

And lastly, is to set up IGTV. This is technically a separate app from Instagram but your most recent IGTV video is highlighted on your Instagram profile. On IGTV, you can upload a recorded video in portrait mode and it will stay on there as long as you keep it up. This is great because followers can look through previous videos and go way back which is not the traditional way Instagram is utilized.

Chapter 10 Action Steps:

- ❏ Follow a minimum of 50 new accounts daily. *Date completed:* _____

- ❏ Create your hot list of your favorite 30 hashtags. *Date completed:* _____
- ❏ Start posting in Instagram Stories once or twice a day. *Date completed:*

_____

❑ Continue to reach out to new prospects
and follow up with warm leads. *Date
completed:* _____

❑ On-going: And don't forget your daily
mindset work implementing journaling,
reviewing your vision board, meditating
and reading educational books!

CHAPTER 11

Automate your Business
with Facebook Groups

*"Tell me and I'll forget. Show me and I may
remember. Involve me and I learn."*
~Benjamin Franklin

I'm super excited about this chapter's content because when you learn how to set up your Facebook group properly and use it as a sales funnel, not only will your team start duplicating rapidly, but you'll also start enjoying the entire process more. Instead of following up over and over with prospects wishing they'd finally watch the video you sent them, you can get them plugged into the culture immediately and eventually wanting more!

Setting Up Your Facebook Group

Unless your upline is already running their group the way I'm going to teach you in this chapter or you love the way it's flowing, I want you to consider creating your own. You'll want to have your team add all of their potential prospects into it so you can start creating instant momentum. Use this script to send so no one is added without knowing it. No one likes that!

"Hey! I just added you to my private Facebook group [Insert Name] – do not feel obligated to stay in it but of course I'd appreciate the support☺. Thank you!"
OR
"Hey! I have a really fun group I run and thought you'd like to check it out. Once you hop in let me know what you think – enjoy!" [give link to the group]

Create a closed group that does not have your company's name in it. Even though it's going to be very obvious what company the group is about, we still want some curiosity around it and not to sound salesy. Pay someone on Fiverr to create a cover photo for the group that is clean and appealing or use Canva to design it.

Adjust the privacy settings so that anyone in the group can add others to it. Make it so that admins or moderators must approve posts – this is a big one! You want to be the admin and you can let a couple of your leaders be moderators.

Content for your Facebook Group

Add at least 5-10 posts to your group before adding anyone else to it. Putting items in the Files tab that are frequently requested are great starting points. Before and after testimonials are always a win and I also find that people love video-based posts too. See what the company has to offer or make your own. Sharing current company sales or incentives are great as well, just make sure you delete them when they're over to keep everyone happy☺.

The focus of your content should be more on the customer side while mixing in opportunities to join the business. I do recommend always leading with the business when first introducing your opportunity to prospects but if they don't jump on board initially we're going to take a softer approach on-going.

In my group, we post once or twice a day and our retention has been extremely high. Some leaders in the industry recommend posting less frequently so experiment with it to see what works for you. Go live once a week or so and rotate with the leaders on your team to increase engagement.

Your Pinned Post

Hands down, creating a strategic pinned post inside of my private Facebook group for my team has been the biggest impact on duplication within my business. We'll talk about the ATM method in a minute, but let's first go over the content to be covered in your pinned post.

The pinned post is basically your featured opportunity video where you will tag prospects and teach your team to do the same. Do a Facebook Live inside of your group and make sure it is no more than 15 minutes in length. Give a quick intro and ask viewers to tag whoever added them to the group and let them know you're going to go over the key products in the line so they can see what's best for them. Go over the benefits of the products and the company and then share before and after testimonials. Showing real pictures is great to do too!

Tell them how they can become a customer, explain your referral program and finish by prompting them to put something in the comments such as more info if they'd like to check out the business side of your company. The person who added them is responsible for tagging them in a video on the business and needs to understand that those are really great prospects.

The Raffle

To get some major momentum going, you can hold a raffle once a quarter. You won't want to do it more than that or your customers will start expecting it and it'll lose some of its excitement. Announce when you're going to share the raffle details on your personal page and inside of your group and have your leaders do the same. Choose a popular product and raffle off at least one item.

Do a Facebook Live on your personal page to kick off the raffle campaign. Ideas to enter the raffle are to share your Facebook Live onto their page, tag some friends in the comment or add people to your private Facebook group (*with their permission of course*). During the Facebook Live, ask viewers to hit share and tag whoever invited them to watch it to enter the raffle. Introduce yourself and why you started using the products. Share 3 to 5 tips in relation to your company's product line and explain again how they can enter the raffle. Tell them the raffle winners will be announced inside of the Facebook group 24 to 48 hours later. Winners must be present to win!

In the raffle winner video (inside of your Facebook group), let them know winners will be announced at the end and you're going to go over the company's most popular products. Have viewers tag whoever invited them. Your video should be no longer than 15 minutes so use that as a guideline to decide which products you will cover. Review your products.

Before you announce the winners, tell them you're going to touch on the business opportunity briefly. Go over the highlights of your company and why it's a great opportunity. Tell them to put more info in the comments and make sure whoever added them to the group tags them on your business opportunity video. Announce the winners! And end with encouraging them to check out the webinar or hop on one if you have any coming up soon.

Variations to the raffle are holding some sort of challenge, hosting an event or even doing an online party within your group. Be creative and remember people love the chance to win free stuff!

The Business Opportunity Webinar

As soon as you're done with the raffle, schedule a webinar and title it something catchy to pique interest on how they can build their business online or something similar to create curiosity. I use Zoom and if you're going to start team calls soon, I'd go ahead and invest in it. Otherwise you could do a Facebook Live instead but a webinar stands out as something special. Raffle something off for this that isn't product-related such as a book.

Start with a quick intro of yourself and ask them to tag whoever invited them to the webinar. Tell them what you'll cover in the webinar: how we leverage social media without being annoying or spammy, the fast start program your company offers and bonuses available (*if applicable*), and how to work through your friends' friends to build a team without bugging or calling people. Whatever their reason for considering the business side, your company can help them get there.

Review the products and company (*utilize a PowerPoint if your company has one*). Show before and after pictures. Explain the power of social sharing and why it works. Tell them you are big on utilizing Facebook groups. Whenever someone has a question, you just add them into the group. It's that simple.

Let viewers know you use the ATM method which means add prospects to the group, tag them in the pinned post, and then message them after they watch it to answer questions. I did not make that method up as its been used in the industry for some time now but it's genius! Share the different ways they can get started (*ie: retail customer, VIP, business builder*) and create urgency by letting them know timing is everything.

Close by directing them to get with the person who invited them and add people to the closed group, then tag them in the pinned post. Announce the raffle winners and say find out how to get started asap!

Chapter 11 Action Steps:

☐ Unless you're going to use your upline's, go ahead and create your own Facebook group for prospects. *Date completed:*

_____

☐ Go through your friends list and use the script included in this module to add 100-300 people to your Facebook group. *Date completed:* _____

☐ Do your Facebook Live pinned post inside of your Facebook group (*if running your own group*). *Date completed:*

_____

☐ Run a raffle contest to drive new people into your Facebook group. *Date completed:* _____

❑ Optional: Schedule your business opportunity webinar. *Date completed:*

_____

❑ On-going: And don't forget your daily mindset work implementing journaling, reviewing your vision board, meditating and reading educational books!

CHAPTER 12

Turning One Customer into Hundreds

"Nothing influences people more than a recommendation from a trusted friend. A trusted referral influences people more than the best broadcast message. A trusted referral is the Holy Grail of advertising."

~Mark Zuckerberg

I think when you first start out in network marketing, you're so eager to find something that works that you try to copy trainers in the industry and sometimes it just doesn't work for you. I've noticed with myself personally that my strength is excellent customer service that overtime has equated to massive amounts of referrals and many upgrades where they've decided to join my team.

No matter if you love leading with the business versus the product, you'll want to make sure you're implementing the steps in this chapter to take great care of your customers and to help your team do the same.

Step 1

As soon as I get a new customer, I immediately write them a handwritten thank you note and drop it in the mail. When was the last time you received a real thank you note in the mail? You will instantly stand out to your customer and they will appreciate the gesture.

Step 2

Have amazing customer service and take care of them right off the bat. Are there any important FAQs or instructions you can either tag them on in a group or email to them directly? Make sure they know how to get in touch with you if they need anything.

Step 3

Create a scheduled follow up system so you know how frequently to check in with them and make sure you don't space out on them. Every other time, make sure you're checking in as a friend if you were friends before your network marketing business. You don't want to be *that* girl who only messages when she wants something, right?

Step 4

Explain your referral program (*or create your own*) and let them know to send anyone to you that may be interested and you'll take care of it from there. We want it to be super easy for them to refer others. If you have some extra samples laying around, ask your customers if they know anyone who would like to try them. Also explain how they can add people to your group if you have one.

Step 5

Ask them to create a curiosity post. When you do get that message from them that they're in love, ask them if they'd be willing to create a post (*with your help*) and that you'll take care of following up with anyone who comments or expresses interest. This works amazingly well so don't be shy about asking!

Step 6

Ask them to host an online 15-minute Facebook party. For a thorough training on the format of these parties, check out my 15 Minute Facebook Party Workshop to learn what to post, how often, how to run the party, etc.

What's really neat about these parties is you can walk away with upwards of 50 leads, several customers and eventually business builders who upgrade. It's pretty incredible!

Step 7

Speaking of upgrading, when you have had a happy customer for several months, you can approach them about joining your team. Just say something such as, *"Hey, Sarah – since you're such a fan of _____, I wanted to see if you'd like to learn more about the business side?"*

Keep it low key when asking your customers because you never want to risk losing an amazing customer just to get a kitnapper. I am not a fan – I'd rather have a raving fan for years vs. a one hit wonder. Agreed?!

Chapter 12 Action Steps:

❑ Put all of your customers together in a notebook or on a spreadsheet and write out your follow up schedule. *Date completed:* _____

❑ Ask one of your current customers to do a curiosity post. *Date completed:*

_____

❑ Optional: Schedule your first Facebook Party (if applicable). *Date completed:*

_____

❑ Go through your current customer list and see who you could approach about your business opportunity. *Date completed:* _____

❑ On-going: And don't forget your daily mindset work implementing journaling, reviewing your vision board, meditating and reading educational books!

CHAPTER 13

Leading by Example

"A good leader inspires people to have confidence in their leader. A great leader inspires people to have confidence in themselves." ~Anonymous

Wow, Goal Diggers! Can you believe we are almost to the end of our time together in this book? Hopefully you've worked through all of the material previous to this chapter so you are ready to embark on the exciting journey of leading others.

When it comes to leadership, we have to be able to "lead" ourselves first so that we can lead others. Here are some of my favorite quotes around the topic but I encourage you to find your own and put it in a cute frame where you can see it often:

"A leader is one who knows the way, goes the way and shows the way."
~John C. Maxwell

"Leadership is not a position or title, it is action and example."
~Ancient Proverb

"If your actions inspire others to dream more, learn more, do more and become more, you are a leader."
~John Quincy Adams

Leading Others

The saying, *"Your vibe attracts your tribe"* is not just a catchy slogan, but a true reflection of your leadership style. We're all leading, whether we realize it or not. My toddler is walking around saying, *"Oh my gosh!"* just like I do as we speak☺. The good news is that if the energy of your team isn't how you'd like to see it, you can change it! Leadership is learned and for you to be reading through this book shows you are committed to learning and growing. It will feel uncomfortable at first but it is *SO* rewarding and definitely an amazing responsibility.

Let's review essential traits you'll want to work on developing:

The Common Characteristics of a Leader (*adopted from* The Huffington Post)

1. Collaborative
2. Visionary
3. Influential
4. Empathetic
5. Innovative
6. Grounded
7. Ethical
8. Passionate

Common Mistakes & Pitfalls

Most everyone that joins the network marketing industry becomes a leader by default. Without proper guidance or coaching, it is *VERY* easy to make these common mistakes. So, if you've experienced any of these issues, it's okay – don't beat yourself up. Remember that hindsight is 20/20 and your goal is to continue to grow every single day, personally and professionally, and to inspire others to do the same! Now let's take a look at the most common mistakes:

❑ Ignores issues
❑ Causes dependency

- ❑ Gives way more than is receiving back (*within reason*)
- ❑ Assuming their new people have "*got it*"
- ❑ Doesn't set clear expectations
- ❑ Bossy
- ❑ Pushing people into ranks
- ❑ Feeds into negativity and drama

Developing a Team

When you hear the phrase, developing a team, what this means essentially is learning how to teach your people to turn around and teach their people. This is the heart of duplication. You can do everything yourself if you try, but it will only get you so far in your business. And it is very stressful! Give people a chance to rise up and you will be amazed at what happens. Here are the key areas to master:

- ♥ Onboarding
- ♥ Holding their hand
- ♥ Teach them to duplicate
- ♥ Constantly affirm

Taprooting

One thing to always keep in mind is that whoever joins your team does not understand leadership and most likely isn't even aware that they have skills they need to develop. There are going to be more times than not that someone joins in your downline and has zero guidance. This can be detrimental for your team and also for their experience with your company.

To proactively address this, implement a taprooting system (*aka leapfrogging*). This is where you reach down into your downline and mentor those that are raising their hand that they want to run or do not have someone properly leading them. Do what you can to work with their direct upline so that they can learn how to develop people under them. However, you will quickly learn who wants to rise up and who doesn't.

I like to reach out to every single new person that joins my team and introduce myself. I give them my personal cell phone and tell them to reach out if they ever need anything. Then I check my numbers daily to see who's truly working the business or who needs support and I *unapologetically* mentor wherever I can.

Recognition and Inspiration

Part of being an exceptional leader is learning how to inspire your team and recognizing those that are working hard. Here are some ideas to get you started!

- √ Create a way for new team members to be welcomed to the group
- √ Make a big deal over rank advancements
- √ Run contests with prizes
- √ Paint a picture of what's possible
- √ Notice the little things
- √ Give them opportunities to lead
- √ Treat them like gold

When to Start Leading

You can start leading immediately. Even if you don't have a team going yet you can find ways to offer value inside of groups or with your social media posts. If you've outgrown your own upline's leadership or have a different leadership philosophy, you can branch off and start your own Facebook groups and/or weekly team calls. It takes quite a bit of effort to run either of these so don't do it just to do it. Make sure you can commit to the consistent effort it takes to launch these and keep them going!

The Four Color Personalities For MLM

Have you ever recruited someone and just couldn't figure them out, or worse, not be able to motivate them? Or have you been having a conversation with a prospect and they seemed interested but then they became silent or said no all of a sudden? This is most likely because they are a completely different color than you so it's your job to learn these well for yourself and for those that you lead!

Yellow "The Helper"

- o Loves giving hugs to strangers
- o Everyone loves them and trusts them

- Not interested in the compensation plan
- Wants to know if the products help people
- Great servant leaders
- Doesn't like being bossed around
- Great at relationships

Blue "Let's Party"
- Loves fun, travel and adventure
- Loves meeting new people
- Talks to everyone, always talking
- Natural promoters, i.e.: *gotta see this movie!*
- Network marketing is a perfect fit
- They don't listen well; mind is going in a million directions
- Not great at following up, too busy meeting new people

Red "Bossy"
- Wants to be in charge
- Organized, tells others what to do
- Wants results, can't stand people whining with excuses

- Will make the most money
- Their way or the highway attitude
- Wants you to get the job done and doesn't want your input
- Gets things done
- Very competitive, loves trophies and recognition

Green "Information"
- Loves data
- Can seem boring to others
- Not much emotion
- Logical, typically wants more info
- Loves spreadsheets, analytics, collecting data and pondering
- Likes to think of all the future scenarios
- Spends too much time thinking vs. taking action
- Wants to be able to answer any question from prospects/team

You'll naturally be drawn to people with similar personalities but will experience tremendous growth when you master leading and developing different personalities. You can find more info from the book The Four Color Personalities for MLM!

Chapter 13 Action Steps:

- ❑ Go through your downline and look up each business builder to see what business they're bringing in. *Date completed:* _____

- ❑ Set up calls with your leaders and go over their goals and help them put a plan together. *Date completed:*

  _____

- ❑ Come up with an incentive contest for your team. *Date completed:*

  _____

- ❑ Determine the dominant color personality of each of your team members. *Date completed:* _____

CHAPTER 14

Now What?

"And I think to myself, what a wonderful world."
~Louis Armstrong

Have you ever found yourself in a situation where there is *SO* much you want to say that you're literally overwhelmed by it and therefore can't think of anything to say?

Fortunately, I'm not to that point, because I love talking and teaching as you know, but I really do wish you could know what I know about you. I know that you are amazing. I know that you are worth the happiness and success you desire. I know that you are absolutely unique and stunning and one-of-a-kind.

But I also know that it doesn't matter what I think. It honestly only matters what you think about yourself and the world around you. For some reason most of us have been taught to play small. To not risk too much so we don't get hurt, look like a failure or make a fool of ourselves.

However, today, I want to challenge you to think differently. To ask yourself, "*What if?*" What if you did go after the goals you wrote down in chapter one and two and really showed up? What if you gave it your all, just to see what you were capable of?

You were drawn to me for a reason. There are no coincidences. Do you think it's possible that I showed you that there is more? That by going after your goals and truly working to crush one after another, you can live the life of your dreams?

It's time to stand up for your dreams. It's time to stand up for your happiness. It's time to fight for your life, look in the mirror and say, "*I want more. I demand more. I am creating more today.*" And literally wash, rise and repeat day after day.

There will be ups and downs. You will have a huge success and the next day get bad news that may bring you to your knees. But as a Goal Digger, you will get back up. You will find yourself inside the ring, fighting and believing and wanting more.

If you truly step into this challenge, you will grow more as a person in a year than you have your entire life. You will be getting closer and closer to the person you were meant to be.

So the question is, ya ready?

Goal Digger *[Noun]: A driven person who's on fire for life and crushing one goal after another.*
~Kimberly Olson

ABOUT THE AUTHOR

Kimberly Olson, PhD, is the creator of *The Goal Digger Girl*, a multi-dimensional brand that serves female entrepreneurs through small group coaching, focused workshops and a whole lot of training on how to build successfully on social media.

She has two PhDs in Natural Health and Holistic Nutrition, has achieved a leadership position in her current network marketing company, has a weekly podcast called *The Goal Digger Girl*, and travels nationally public speaking.

She is a busy mom of two and lives in Austin, Texas with her husband, Scott. Her favorite thing about being an entrepreneur is being able to take care of her family while building an incredible business. And of course, she also loves teaching others how to follow their dreams, crush their goals and create the life they've always wanted.

Stay Connected 🤍

Facebook *@TheGoalDiggerGirl*

Instagram *@TheGoalDiggerGirl*

LinkedIn *@TheGoalDiggerGirl*

YouTube *@TheGoalDiggerGirl*

Pinterest *@GoalDiggerGirl*

Twitter *@Goal_DiggerGirl*

TheGoalDiggerGirl.com